For Art & Helen –

with all best wishes,

Robert

Albuq.
June 1985

Books by Robert Peterson

Home for the Night
The Binnacle
Wondering Where You Are
Under Sealed Orders
Lone Rider
Leaving Taos
The Only Piano Player in La Paz

THE ONLY PIANO PLAYER

IN

LA PAZ

Robert Peterson

Black Dog Press
1985

Acknowledgments

Grateful acknowledgment is made to the following publications in which these poems first appeared:

kayak: Leadville, Colo.: Scattering Aunt's Ashes; Yellow Ferry Harbor, Sausalito; La Paz

Hubbub: Costs; A Gift; A Critic

New: How To Get On Italian Trains

Northwest Review: Geography

PinchPenny: Letters To The Editor: 12 Redactions

Poetry Northwest: Kicking It Around With Spats Longo, a Serious Contender

Tyuonhi: Theme and Variations after Yannis Ritsos; Second Variation on a Theme by Ritsos; Third Variation on a Theme by Ritsos

Mark In Time: Wingwalking in Oregon

First Printing, 1985

Printed in the United States of America

Published by Black Dog Press
P.O. Box 1213
Capitola, California 95010

ISBN 0-933525-25-7
Library of Congress Catalog Card Number 85-70518

Contents

Beauty and terror are very real things.

G. K. CHESTERTON

How To Get On Italian Trains

A Critic

My card, sir.
You already know who you are.

My compliments to your palmist, & your aperçu machine.

But you deserve most of the credit, really.
Only great jokers

Can strike smart poses
by telescopes

in planetariums.

And precious few of these can speak
as you do

in spoons, tacks, & triangles.

Ghazal for the Eclipse

Gaining ground through smoked salmon & sinister martinis
I suddenly notice an alarming loss of weight in the old table.

A sentimental dream of graft in the string section.
In the curvature of sleep, we continue to compare
bright & dark regions.

Watching la luna disappear in shadowy silence.
Observed in silence. The same laws apply to clocks & kings.

Thinking of the manic Slav, with fine wrist bones, whose eyebrows
vanish at dawn. "Gin did not just happen by chance," she says.

O, give us cool competitors who can consistently keep the ball low.
As moonlight returns to the sleek silos in Nebraska, & my clothes.

Robert's Rules of Order

for Ann Steinmetz

"A group of 37 Scouts and 3 leaders left Thursday on a 22-day excursion that will include gold-panning in New Mexico mountain streams. They are headed for the Scout Ranch near Cimarron, N.M. but will stop en route at Hearst Castle, and Disneyland."

Troop 51 those days
you put your fire-engine-red name button on the Official beanie
& sang off to Camp Roy-ah-nay.
Smoked basket reeds. Drank bug juice. Got poison oak & sunburn.
Wrote Mom for more clean underwear & cookies, & a hunting knife
just like Jack's.

Bored by bugles, badges, leaders
& the whole Mary Ann, came home early
put on old cords
to see some Saturday Westerns.

Panning for gold in Cimarron
based on universality of acquisitive instincts
& out of our jurisdiction.

Disneyland we enjoyed
functioning as independent intoxicated adult unit
but only partly outdoors
in any event not probative to Being Prepared
therefore overruled.

Hearst Castle: granted indefinite continuance.

What we see is a bunch of jive; bogus sunshine —
Sammy Davis, Jr. trying to play *Othello*.

I'm in there, we go Southwest
swearing beer, Pepsi cans out of trout streams
milk a couple elk
throw a few strings firecrackers into Lama Foundation
miss bad old mountains by minutes

then hot-foot them sleepy small-town magistrates

Wingwalking in Oregon

Last Sunday petrified
on Bridal Veil, a beginner's climb,
trail no wider than a carton of Kents.
Nice cliff & Eiffel view
for families
fresh from church. But
goosed by heights, how can I
embrace the sublime
without a priest
& no goddam fence?

Now
Saddle Mountain,
called benign.
Trail this time
half a loaf of bread
and the scenery true

Now I'm looking over edge
of Oregon
into depths of Idaho & potatoes,
breadcrumbs, birds, diseases of birds,
starch in the blood, playground donkeys,
slides, songs & other conveyances
of childhood

If somehow
I let go
& spider safely down
concentrated & green
what will I remember
but above all
to whom can I complain?

What I Worried, Getting Here

I hear it rains funerals in Palermo.

Wiser men are gaffed in Naples.
Should I make a scene
or fly quietly northeast, according to plan?

What is the average courage required
to tour Pompeii publicly
for erotic reasons?

Will long hours of leisure & lasagna
in crumbling towns bargaining for rugs with smiles
be seen by my aunt
as time well-spent?

"You're not getting any younger," she says.
"And look rather pale."
She's pushing the fish in Alaska.
That's the thinking in Colorado.

Advised to change trains in Fossano
I lose Fossano. A Greek in cuban heels
nicks my sandals.

Do real boats become paper boats
when the moon shines
on party hats?

Too late to turn back.
Pray we're met promptly at the pier
by amiable officials

And a fleet friend who knows.

How To Get On Italian Trains

Here we are in italy seized with a classic romantic or practical
destination. We are taken to the Stazione to look for
Informazione.

Treno numero uno will depart for Lucca at fourteen thirty-two
on binario numero quatro. Ordinarily binario would be in italics
but italy these days

Is no ordinary place. There may be an earlier treno, but we don't know
this because we didn't ask. Anyway we proceed to Billeti & manage
to talk up a ticketo.

Time for a sandwich or drink. Actually much more time
but we don't know this. But if you're like some italians
even if you *are* italian

You're out on the binario early, to see what is going to happen.
And don't try to pretend we're not waiting for the treno because
that's what's done these days en route to

Savona, Imperia, Roma, Firenze, Bari, Cipressa or Milano. Later
perhaps
we *will* get to Milano. At the moment we're looking for the direttissimo
to Lucca.

A voice from the systemo: Attenzione: treno, thirty minuti en re-
tardo. We take this in stride like an experienced traveler
strolling up & down the platform

Wondering if Sandy Koufax will make Hall of Fame this year.
Finally, ecco el treno. All aboard! Jostle, push, elbow, bump, kick
& shove. Treno doors are small & the corridors narrow.

Never attempt to get on italian trains under the influence
or with more than
one suitcase, unless you want to risk
being trampled to morto.

So here we are, the surviving passageri
bustling & banging back & forth
looking for a posto, shoving bags & baskets & jugs of vino
& parcels of vittles
this way & that

Like any normal crowd of sons of bitches shooting to kill
to get comfortable. And we are fighting for a posto
in a compartamento
for men only

Because nine times out of ten ladies on trenos
have bambini & lots of candy, capice? So here we are, bene.
The confusione subsides temporarily. Avanti!

We've already missed our connection at La Spezia. But let us proceed
somehow, as promised, to Milano — Milano with its vast, acoustically
perfecto Stazione

Not as big as Grand Central or the Coliseum, or Meteor Crater
Arizona, but big enough to moor a few dirigibles in
— not a bad idea.

At Easter all Milanese go to Genova & all the Genovese
treno to Milano. Not necessarily by train of course. Anyway in Milano
one does not breathe deeply on binarios

Because of dense clouds of poisonous fumes which this giant città
famous in earlier time for opera, produces. In an hour or so (or
tomorrow?) we leave Milano for Trieste.

Finally, el capo de Stazione, wearing his jaunty red cap
(mistaken by many beginners for a taxi driver)
waves his wand, & away we go, fifty minuti en retardo.

Leaving Genova, that is. This about covers getting on italian trains.
Getting off is essentially the same
unless you arrive in the wrong town.
Tomorrow, or the day after
we discuss how to send, or receive, an italian telegram.

Old Pop

won't stop TALKING, feels the milk,
bran & yogurt in his blood, ready or not
he's got to

get going, look after Property
& Loved Ones, mend moth-holes
in the old tarpaulin, compose

Morning Dispatches, too busy
to raise shades
or change pajamas, it's

Lectures for panhandlers
& peanut-vendors
the spine must be kept in line

And the whole glorious story
invulnerable to onslaughts of fact, told
in its entirety according to

Jubilees
of Notes
& Experiences — practicing locution

Stone-deaf in a bathtub,
demonstrating the Fitzimmons Shift,
driving Lady Lily out of the house

Into Tijuana sailor dives
for a little peace & quiet . . .

Capricorn is rising, the third eye
of Texas
Open for Business

It's his deal
cards are falling just right
& it's ABOUT TIME

Leadville, Colo.: Scattering Aunt's Ashes

(Althea Crawford, 1894-1974)

Harrison Avenue, frigid May morning: Honda, Utah plate
white helmet on handlebars
front yard of 817, last frame house this end
of the street. My grandfather Edward's house.

Masonic cemetery goes on & on, a long time
finding the markers — Edward & Martha's
among dry weeds & patches of ice.
Or, seems like a long time.

Open the package — size, weight of a traveler's clock
with a trout knife. Tap her clean, on a low, respectful
angle
close to ground.

Galosh, mitten, steam-breath, my red sled. Bakery smells
of the assay office on 2nd Street.
Keeping a promise made in Oregon.
My idea. She couldn't have cared less.

Mt. Elbert, deep snow. Springtime a month off yet
in Lake County.

Baby Doe Bar, the waitress is friendly.
"Up from Taos to fish. But too early, too cold.
I was a kid here."
She's got a figure. We make a date.

But something craven couldn't wait. I ran for Salida, & home.
And that was it.

Amos Feely at the Fielding

Room service every two hours: two beers.
All night, all day.

Lotused on the bed like a skinny guru in BVD's
reading the papers, nothing but papers
all day, all night.

A dollar tip for every bell. Mornings,
empties in neat lines outside the door.
The maid takes them away, knocks once, leaves
clean linen.

After 10 days, no more, no less, the same
grilled ham and cheese on rye at midnight
morning train, Vancouver or Detroit.

He traveled for a big union, father said.
Paid every bill on the dot.
The lobby-sitters wondered.
A widower, mother thought.

Fifty, say. Never phoned, or met a soul.
Hated radios, planes, & lobby-sitters.
Lived in his hornrims, his Millers, his papers.

Never slept, or bothered, or talked.
Amos, some were sad for you. I was not.

Paul's Minute Waltz

for P.S.

Allegro vivace

thin as ladles
soft as cradles

mean as rats
smart as hats

tough as a knuckle
below the buckle

bald as nails
hairy as tails
sexy as veils

fast as bats
slow as chats

short as bubbles
long as huddles

powdered as frumps
patched as tramps

fresh as spray
sweet as hay

as a bird is to twig
as beer is to swig
as small is to big

safe as houses
blue as noses

toothed as a law
locked as a jaw

cruel the lash
kinder the cash

drink up
and keep it simple

look smart
and smile a dimple

lights out
and bob's your uncle

Kicking It Around With Spats Longo,
a Serious Contender

for M. A. Ashley

Gothic, you want gothic? O.K., here's La Vona Osling
of Manteca, & her no-good son BoBo Minardi
the Salinas Streak —

Unknown Soldier of the oud & ocarina.

Then Voodoo Mama of Stockton.
And Sacramento Bob, transcendentalist & haywire skydiver.
We won't even mention Fred Lusk, that dimp

who tried to convert his Studebaker into a Ranchero.

I'm sorry your sense of humor's slipped like a cheap ring
down between the sofa-cushions.
But moderation was never your middle name, Slick.

Just don't worry. You don't want your face to freeze that way.
Remember you are, at all times, the flip side
of yourself.

Keep punching, & keep your Marx & Trotsky handy.

What you really want to do, I know
is sweep the unsuspecting reader like a lace doily or bay leaf
into the maelstrom, without a struggle.

And that's what you do, pal. Olé!
Because of you, & you only, all the stars & planets
have new, sensible names like Mel, Sue, Buck, & Jim-Bob

which makes them more close & personal.

Passing the time till important calls & appointments
with gum-ball chores like pricing jello or counting grapes
is, I agree, nothing to be ashamed of.

But who can fade trick questions like
"Do you file?"
Enough to remind the most neutral observer
of Fred Lusk's eggshell socks

or mudslides & facelifts.

Then Spike, that low-slung streetfighter
got a ticket to cat-Siberia
for being such a nightly nuisance

But came around to bump heads while you were brooding
in the herb garden
& now's a great big sweetheart, right?

You turn up treasures no one else would touch with a nine-foot pole.

Speaking as your lazy river of advice
I understand completely how going with the flow
makes you cringe & wince, kid.

But even if you feel cheezy or faint
it's always better to sit & draw toads
& frauds than not draw at all.

Thumbs up! You're clear for takeoff. Contact!

Call it roadwork, or a searchlight.
A bluebird, pard.
The midnight special, yeah — on the Rock Island Line.

History, Almost

"I am always acutely conscious of the ludicrous quality of the past."

Jean Dutourd

A film, the best & worst of the silents
& I don't agree with the editor

or my date has a wild idea relating to other transactions
& we sit through it twice

Or, years earlier I can't get a date & stay home
in my armor, lonely as a goalie.

As time allows, we cling to our little notebooks, adrift
in the overloaded lifeboat:

The horse, the old family horse pulling the cart to market.
Later, a great white one outracing the corrupt revolution.

A smart crowd of kings & queens, yes, & their forthcoming
knights, & just enough fine steeds & swords
arrayed under a full moon

In authentic costumes
A hot director & choreographer ready to roll,
that's it tomorrow.

Enough, at least, to get us to the next station, or moon.
Dodging maniacs on the road. Thanking the stars.
Knocking the worst villains on their heads.

Naturally the cat yawns
reminding of a woman, face forgotten
but every movement remembered perfectly.

You lift a prima ballerina easily with one hand
to the sound of chuckling kites, & sawmills

As the snow, the snow of the moment
vanishes over the lake.

Onward If Not Upward

For every man
risking it all
on a mountain

Only because
it's vertical
as well as available

There has to be one
at least as heroic

Who couldn't care less
for exactly the same reasons

Which explains, doesn't it, why
so many august personages
& equestrian statues

Historical landmarks
& memorial rotundas

Are
what they are

Not to mention
the occasional maharajah
or mule

Who just sits there?

Confidence

I watch her
        as she sleeps

her breathing as even
        as the lines

in telegrams

her chest rising and falling
        like Arcaro

winning at Jamaica
        by six lengths

and know
        as her lashes

flutter once

then twice, the dreams
        are all good

and all
        of me.

Letters To The Editor: 12 Redactions

1.

I have a B.A. in journalism.
And writing is my favorite pastime.

I've done so many poems
it's impossible
to single out just one
as being the best.

They are all in that category.

My poems come in several different styles.
But this one
is a love poem.

More are available on demand.

2.

I am a New Poet.

Never thought I'd write poetry
        even though I always loved it.
But I had *no say in all this!*

It came to me as if dictated
        from "God knows where."

I was about to cook supper
when suddenly
whole sentences rushed into my head
        — all in rhyme.

I quickly called my daughter
to take over
        (big deal — hot dogs & beans!)

As she looked at me, totally puzzled,
I wrote these things down.

Well, I thought, if all this
        is worth its salt
it will be revealed.

From then on, things began to drop into place.
I found a workshop in a college.

"Velma, you've got talent!" the teacher said.

3.

I have become a local legend in Salem
for some reason.

I was a stripper by the name of
"Princess Shoshone"

who received oodles of media coverage.

Mostly because of my upper middle class background.

("Why *was* this girl stripping?")

In fact, the job exposed me
to other levels of existence
I otherwise
would never have seen.

So, I am currently wrapped up
in composing
my Autobiography.

I want to clarify things
for myself
& organize
my inner growth.

4.

I have been writing poems for many years.
I have over 100 good ones!

I also have 50 songs, many to tunes of old-time songs
such as

"When My Blue Moon Turns to Gold Again"
                        and
"What a Friend We Have in Jesus."

"Send only one poem," you said. So! I am sending one poem
and the names of 62 others.

Most, like "The Groceryman's Prayer," "What Is a Smile?" and
"Can God Tell a Lie?" are about people.

Others, like "Dad's Cigar," and "Cats and Tobacco"
are about tobacco.

5.

I can write twenty poems
or whatever I feel like that day
in less than two days.

I wrote MY EXISTENCE
on April Fools Day, 1983
in twenty minutes.

Accounting is my profession.
I've had no training in anything.

Thanks for your time.

6.

A few years ago when I was about 16, 17
or 18 years old (around '76, or '77)
that's when I wrote this poem.

I was depressed. So I went to my room
& started writing.

I'm not going to tell you how old I am
but I will tell you I was born
around 1960.

I don't think this makes much sense.
It's more like an ad-lib
from a Marx Brothers movie.

I hope you like it.
But if you don't, that's just fine with me.

7.

I am a 12-year-old boy
interested in becoming a writer.

I write stories & poems.

Just because I don't get them published
doesn't mean
I'm not a writer.

After all, I wrote them!

I'm sorry this poem isn't typed.
I can't afford one yet.

I saw your ad in *Writer's Digest*
to which I subscribe.

By the way, I get no help, *whatsoever*
from my parents.

8.

Family worship should be a joyful, happy time for children.
Not just something for them to "endure."

It's a wonderful experience to watch the spiritual development
of children

PLANNED FOR THEIR PARTICULAR AGE LEVEL!

Our Kevin
already an enthusiastic soul-winner at 12
puts it this way:

> "Since we started having family worship
> in our home
> I have finally found the courage
> to witness for the Lord."

He lists three benefits
that have come to him
through family worship:

> 1. I am more faithful in my prayer life.
> 2. It gives me a hunger for READING THE BIBLE.
> 3. It gives me a burden for lost souls.

Though we do not guarantee
that a few years of family worship
will produce poetry as good as Kevin's
at age 12

The child will certainly read better.
And, in general, understand what he reads.

He will be far, far ahead of his non-worshipping peers
for this experience.

9.

Heaving & groaning
to stay above the blackness
of this treacherous city life.

And my lungs have been expanding
from swimming lessons.

I stay in the apartment more often
instead of running from one coffee house
to the next.

Beyond, I can see daylight
as a writer.

But haven't yet reached the true free space
above the ocean breezes.

This poem, "Alcatraz," will, I hope, make history.

I do not intend it to be subversive, but rehabilitative.
The system is already subversive.

10.

I have written a light Romance.
The manuscript is about 60,350 words.
It is about a dream coming true

But not without the pitfalls life deals out.

I believe this story will sell, because anyone
can relate to the characters.

You will laugh with their joy
& cry for their agony.

No story would be complete without a ghost, of course.
So my Reggie gives the story humor.
He is really such a dear, you have to love him.

I know my characters can prove themselves. But
"It's not quite what we're looking for,"

The publishers seem to be saying.

11.

I would like to discredit some of the charges brought against me.
I will be as brief as possible.

I am not a member of any church.
Nor am I an atheist.

If you are testing the morals of my work, I suggest
you use the Book of Solomon as a reference.

I do not believe in homosexual sex. Nor have I indulged.
I have had no sexual indulgence whatsoever. I write of
the *spirit* of love.

I do not steal my ideas from other books.
I have studied classic verse for 25 years.

I am neither ignorant or depraved.

In an aptitude test, I qualified as a genius. I have that capacity.
This test was administered by Emma O. Jenkins,
in Davis Grammar School,
in 1943.

All my expenses are met by check.
And I can prove the amounts spent.

I don't mind saying, I could use a little Christian tenderness
for a change.
My world seems entirely devoid of it.

12.

Thank you for the invitation.

Enclosed, a poem for your contest.

I hope I win.

But I have never won anything.

In reply to your question

"Do I know some people out there

in Anselmo, Nebraska

who write?"

My answer is

No, I don't.

I don't know anyone.

The Only Piano Player In La Paz

Yellow Ferry Harbor, Sausalito

Never saw a wild duck in a nest before.

And I'm looking this one in the eye.
Entertaining your fuchsias & marigolds with opera
Sunday morning
when I first found her
in a bottle-brush planter
the top of your gangway
— a spot of meditating Mallard gray
gazing serenely south
across the Bay.

Later, I made a count.
Celebrated with your fine Chablis.

But next evening, dismay: everything gone. Just a mess
of feathers. Brought this news to a party
which surprised no one. "A flying fish got them," someone said.
"Or a gull, or some kids. That's the way the world is."

Thought it might be because a former friend
claims I'm untrustworthy. Or because disappointment
has a life of its own.

But this morning, she's home, & I'm on the phone: those feathers
— put down, composed one by one
to fool the flying fish, the gulls, the Generals
& me.

Here she is, as still as a duck
on eight eggs.
Another way the world can be.

Call her Mabel. And when they hatch, before they sail
name one for me.

Geography

Feeding ducks is like a trip to Venice.
Which has never appealed to me, particularly.
I've had better times
in Athens & Copenhagen.

Anyway, here they come, curious & polite
as little motorboats.
I toss the crumbs
like a young democrat

Allowing just enough lead-time
for dilettantes
& slow thinkers.
But when

Those pushy guys, the gulls arrive
cab-drivers from New York & Naples
(ravenous, & unionized)
the honeymoon's over.

Emotion & conflict. Remember when
we went at it in the only decent place
in Barstow, over arms control
& Yankee management?

Another time
right up this street
I won a smart poker hand
& you called me a poor winner.

Finally, late as usual
these café intellectuals
we call goose, gander, geese
up to here

In all that razoo
over atmosphere, priorities, art
& wine.
We might as well be breaking up in France.

Love

Shaving off the moustache is like buying a new hat.

Buying a new hat's like promising to take Maria
to Bermuda.

I did take her to Santa Fé, but well that's life
she's happy now with someone else.

Maybe I'll keep the moustache
combine it with a telltale beard.

White for hope, like a baseball in April
fresh from an umpire's pocket.

Or white for almost anything, like foam, or miniver, or
a sheet of Mead like this

You can write poems on.
You *or* me. It doesn't really matter.

I'll wax & polish them as the meadow turns green
sure as an Irish hat

As we wait like poor mechanics for the moon.

But oh, we have no poor mechanics!
All right, luv. Your way then: Neapolitans.

Costs

for M. K-W.

O peachy, when we ran with the same psychiatrist.
The one with a dream of learning jazz trombone, Suzuki method.

But I fell from favor. She objected to my "childish positions
on forgetfulness & disrespect."

You faithfully kept your appointments downtown.
I forged a new identity in Arrow shirts & karate.

Another winter crossed the line, on a clumsy backstroke.
We made the usual seasonal adjustments.

I threw raindrops at your perms. You pressed weeds in dime novels
& practiced a yard-sale calculator.

Then you stole a library card, & began to act uppity,
frequenting public game rooms & spas

Confronting total, dismal strangers with emotional questions
concerning funerals, bribery, & photosynthesis.

I couldn't be bothered. But if we still cared, according to the customs
of pain, something had to be done.

Maybe it was, maybe it wasn't.
The narrator changed hands.

And a single flight of pelicans became your only consolation.
So far, no adult witness has come forward.

Themes and Variations

after Yannis Ritsos

What you call patience or self-denial, laughter or ambition,
what you call your wayward song
the only song that will make them weaken
& agree without a moment's hesitation
to reveal the amazing truth of the whole matter

is only the silent half of a rose
a hairbreadth beneath the surface
of the prayers, the nameless trifles

& the damp jargon of necessary evasions.

Second Variation on a Theme by Ritsos

Such ghosts, the dawns —
loitering past all hope & fear
                in moonstone gowns
on the grand staircase of memory.

So it is the bright fixed eye
                of a swift train at night
sweeps the closed faces
                of sleeping towns

never once
to look back

on old games & forms
or risk the dark pleas of their dreams.

Third Variation on a Theme by Ritsos

Because the letter from an unknown correspondent is somehow
                                                    interrupted
Because too many eager volunteers arrive for a manhunt
Because dexterity of the magician with tame doves & trunks
Because wise cats & larks appear & disappear as they please
Because of your splendid ignorance of the game
Because of my fascination with elusive shadows of the contestants
Because a confused bamboo chime knocks in the wind, to its true
                                                    nature
Because yesterday's sky was never as close as it seemed
Because even fast friendship can turn white overnight
Because, even so, our first evening star softens immediate sorrow

Because of all this, I ask you to trust me, trust me —
Not to think of what we should have done.

Owl

Norman Disher, poet, builder, hang-glider, 1926-1975

Dawn run off Jeffers' hurt-hawk cliff

That delicious downdraft
no more than a satisfying
snuff-sneeze
by some ancient Norse god of Mischief
& you sang along

When you lost it
went in
with a so-what shrug saying Om Ah
Caramba
that kind
of nonsense

This bird my cat got
both wings neatly in place
not a mark of pain on him
still warm, deadpan
takes me to you, too

Who took sleep when it came
but even awake
one eye wise & the other
wise & private, maybe
you only drifted off there in the air
as you used to
in literary bars
& ice cream parlors

But you looked, they say, "surprised"
I keep remembering that, & a life
from poems to jazz piano to electrons
(& finally, astronomy)
you made look easy

Maybe that final expression
your way to say
not to worry
it's no big deal

Playing Mulligan's "Funny Valentine"
his smoky sidelong horn behind the words
"laughable" & "unphotographable"
that crazy rhyme off the high board

We always claimed we jointly owned
because it proved
anything was possible

Just as I knew
you'd always be around
because only you
were never afraid
to take one more bow
& sing it again

Rio del Mar

Those first great waves, noumenons of sleep, or loss, or flight.
Then ah, that glittering gambler, later on
who strode like a king through my mind

Just as we loved, in our prime.

When the sun ran down, we dawdled home
by wandering wood, small pools of desire, & starlight.

Towards the end, one phantom, I recall
for dark reasons of its own
masked as a god

Broke sighing in the dusk, on a hidden crown.

I lie now in wonder, at dawn
alone by a sea
known only by another, silent sea

More yours than mine.

La Paz

*"This is what love comes down to —
things that happen, and what we say about them."*

Don DeLillo

Side by side, in ornate iron chairs
we amused ourselves with sad affairs
of a wealthy adventuress.

And random, comic voices from an offshore yacht
with nowhere to go
that posed, like a smart model, for every dawn & sunset.

For a heartbeat, I was stupidly angry at a fly
& a lover in another country, long ago.
"Ah, Turner's light," you said (you didn't know).

Darkness.
Somewhere a phone rang twice, then stopped.
A woman laughed. And so, in rum, did we.

When you struck a match, for calm, or time
it was like a cry of praise from home
for patience, & forgiveness.

Recovering From Divorce

Groping for Gabrielli
in the record rack
I discover
the jacket containing overtures
to "Alcina" & "Berenice"
(Boyd Neel conducting the Boyd Neel Orchestra)

does not take me to Boyd Neel, or evocations
of carnal pleasure
or Handel

but only a Mercury LP

Rhumba With Machito

we never got around
to dancing

A Gift

Thank you, Ernesto, for the thank-you note.
Once again I'll say the wedding glowed.

You say the bowl is "unquestionably beautiful."
That was the idea: something beautiful & useful.

Even though presents aren't all that important.
When I got married the first time in Reno

We didn't get any (eloped). Moreover
who gets which present

Can be a source of woe if (god forbid)
things don't, shall we say, go well.

My first thought was to give you (the happy couple)
a big German carving knife; you're both great cooks.

Then I heard this could bring bad luck.
So I hope you get all the sharp things you need

From others
who don't know this.

But it appears the wooden bowl was misinterpreted
Perhaps because it was imported.

Too small for salad, too big for nuts.
You say you don't know what to do with it.

I admit we have a problem. But it's almost as difficult
to explain a wooden bowl

As matrimony, or a snowshoe.
Maybe they are different aspects of the same thing.

Perhaps it's only a matter of numbers.
Would it help

If I sent one more
exactly like the first one?

April, USA, A.D.

1.

The hummingbird hangs like a fire opal
near the begonias
then hesitates a beat
by a pale white rose.

My neighbor the mechanic, the mumbler
trips his man-eating radio: thump-thumping so loud
I can't hear my own Stravinsky.

A surfing mob zombies by
on muscle-trucks & cycles
that remind me
of Magnum .357s.

Young mothers in the emporiums, addled & stained
so spaced from their get
you have to believe love's become
one of the black arts.

Day in, day out, that parlous actor
spit-shines the prim religion
of this winking, war-loving kingdom.

2.

My hummingbird's back.
The same one? Perhaps.
(What can we really prove, or own?)
Certainly not the same country I was born in.

Anyway, the kind of great spring day
you want to live up to.

Let go all failure & blame
lie back on a lawn with cool wine
& perfectly normal urges
to cheat, slander, stab & strangle

And try to take things as they come.

In One Rain

Squall at dusk: solitary souls
of every persuasion
staring moodily out the windows
of lighthouses
poems
a jail

Damp bachelor, beaten again
by his judo umbrella

Dreams
one more
warm embrace

Humming with high valence, virtue
intricate whims & toe, Persian eye
a nose for the ages
& what leg

Sloshed to five winds in manna & gusto
we factor the velocity of a twin-dream
by flickering nordic accents
& circular, half-oriental gesture

Immune
to intimations
of contentment
& oblivion

Finally, as time wanders by
somewhere between one knee & our chins
we sleep like starfish, like children

Like spirits of fire
like iron.

Beach

The shell I picked up, that last day:
Till then, only a common sea we thought might provide
And a cartoon of its tipsy heart, half-gone
in the sand.

You listened, & heard nothing;
You'd wear it, perhaps, someday,
So you said, but you won't.

I could have pretended to hear the coin of that hour,
a river, or a bell, even a bad opera
just to be different, or mad,

Just to be found again, wanting.

The Only Piano Player In La Paz

1.

Soft-shoe of the non-violent pajama: foxtrots
& rockabyes
in the onion soup
of sleep.

Sighing uncles of love
pulsing
like fat accordions, like chaperones
in the veins.

That electric rail, denial.

Scarecrows, subways
& rumbling trestles
of the brain.

2.

I want the simplest thought
to glow like neon

As it speeds through a heart
in the bodies of butterflies;

The storms of revelation
to break

Again & again

On the sly reefs
of your breasts.

I want a jury of our peers, the trees.
I want to hear truth crack its knuckles.

Set at Resource Graphics, San Jose,
in 10 point Century Schoolbook.
Printed by BookCrafters.
Designed by Paul Schofield and the author
in Santa Cruz, California.

Gothic runes selected and drawn by the author.